MW00720417

LOADS AND LOADS OF LIMERICKS

LOADS AND LOADS OF LIMERICKS

Collected by David G. Harris
(who, sadly, does not come from Paris)
Original limericks by the same

Illustrated by Allan Stomann

ANGUS
& ROBERTSON
PUBLISHERS

Contents

Here's loads and loads of limericks,
Those crazy rhyming gimmericks;
    They look easy to write,
    But try some tonight,
And you'll find that the last lines are often impossible.

8

There was a young girl in a bog,
Met a prince who was perched on a log.
    She gave him a kiss
    Which for her was sheer bliss,
But the prince just turned into a frog.

A greedy young fellow named Ned
Ate a feast before going to bed:
    Six lobsters, one ham,
    Then pickles with jam,
And when he woke up he was dead.

9

There is a young lady whose eyes
Are as big as a pair of meat pies.
  Her house and garage,
  Although very large,
Are flooded whenever she cries.

A lady while dining at Kew
Found a fat cabbage moth in her stew.
  Said the waiter, "Don't shout,
  And wave it about,
Or the others will all want one too!"

A cheerful old bear at the zoo
Could always find something to do;
  When it bored him to go
  On a walk to and fro
He reversed it and walked fro and to.

There was an old man up a tree,
Was bit on the nose by a bee;
  So he bandaged his head
  And went off to bed,
But it bit him once more on the knee.*

*Publisher's note: It was of course a different
bee, but the man was in no state
to check such details.

10

There was an old man of the Nile
Whose behaviour was awfully vile.
He would pick at his nose
With two of his toes,
Then belch very loudly and smile.*

*Publisher's note: He was rarely invited to dinner.

There was an old dwarf from Bengal,
From his horse had a terrible fall.
He was split right in two,
But with very strong glue
They mended that man very small.

11

There was a young lady called Wyatt
Whose voice grew incredibly quiet,
Till finally one day,
It just faded away . . .

There is a young girl from Peru
Whose limericks end at line two . . .

There was a young man from Verdun . . .

There once was a baker named Jake
Who stumbled whilst mixing a cake.
  His wife cooked the lot
  In the oven so hot,
And gobbled him up by mistake.*

*Publisher's note: Nutritionists advise checking cake mixture
for foreign bodies before cooking and certainly
before eating. Legal authorities advise checking wills
if contemplating a fate similar to Jake's
for members of your family.

There was a young lady of Russia
Who screamed so that no-one could hush her.
  The noise was so bad
  That her husband went mad,
And at last down the loo tried to flush her.*

*Publisher's note: Plumbers advise that foreign objects
can easily lead to pipe blockages.

There was a young lady from Smyrna
Whose grandmother threatened to burn her;
    So she opened the oven,
    Gave her granny a shove in,
And said with a laugh, "That'll learn ya!"*

*Publisher's note: The Society for the Protection of Grandmothers
has drawn our attention to the young lady's shocking
use of English. They suggest that the grandmother's threat
was probably made in an attempt to encourage her
grand-daughter to speak more correctly. Unfortunately, due to her
untimely cremation, the granny concerned was unavailable for comment.

There was a young lady from Melbourne
Who had a remarkable kidney.
    When they said, "Your address
    Makes this limerick a mess,"
She replied, "But I once lived in Sydney!"

14

There was an old geezer from Gretna
Who fell down the crater of Etna.
   When asked, "Is it hot?"
   He replied, "Is it what!
You could fry a great egg here, I'll bet ya!"*

*Publisher's note: It is more than likely that this
old geezer went to the same school as the
girl from Smyrna.

Moaned a young dinosaur known as Brett,
On a trip to his neighbourhood vet,
   "A curator named Jones
   Offered cash for my bones,
When it's plain that I'm not extinct yet!"

15

A young zoological scholar
Bought an old chimpanzee for a dollar;
But the monkey one night
Set the whole house alight,
Which made him hot under the collar.

There was a young lady named Bright
Whose speed was much faster than light.
She went out one day,
In a relative way,
And returned on the previous night.

16

There was a fat lady from Rye
Who felt she was likely to die,
   And she feared that when dead
   She would not be well fed;
So she gulped down a roast, three chickens,
a ham, twelve buns, a seven-layer cake, four
cups of coffee, and a green apple pie.

An elegant lady from Spain
Was caught in a deluge of rain.
   She was swept off her feet
   And washed down the street,
Then she disappeared down a large drain.

17

A cannibal chief of Penzance
Ate his uncle and two of his aunts;
   He swallowed his mother
   And half of his brother,
And now he can't do up his pants.

18

My very best girlfriend named Maggie
Owned a dog which was awfully shaggy.
   His front end would growl
   And at night it would howl,
But the tail end was friendly and waggy.

There was a young woman of Niger
Who smiled as she rode on a tiger.
   They returned from their ride
   With the lady inside
And the smile on the face of the tiger.

A curious bird is the pelican:
His bill can hold more than his belican.
   He can hold in his beak
   Enough food for a week;
I'm darned if I know how the helican!

As a beauty, I'm not a great star,
There are others more handsome by far;
   But my face, I don't mind it,
   Because I'm behind it —
'Tis the folks in the front that I jar.

There was a young boy from Quebec
Who was buried in snow to his neck.
   When asked, "Are you frizz?"
   He replied, "Yes, I is,
But we don't call this cold in Quebec."

There was a young fellow named Hall
Who fell in the spring in the Fall.
'T'would have been a sad thing,
Had he died in the Spring,
But he didn't—he died in the fall.

There was a young man from Taree
Who went fancy dress as a tree;
But his trouble began,
This poor little man,
When a very large dog tried to pee.

I wish that my room had a floor,
I don't care as much for a door;
   But this walking around
   Without touching the ground
Is getting to be such a bore.

I'd rather have fingers than toes,
And I'd rather have feet than a nose;
   But as for my hair,
   I'm glad that it's there
And I'll be very sad when it goes.

22

A crazy young student from Shoreham
Made brown paper trousers and wore 'em.
　　He looked nice and neat
　　Till he bent in the street
To pick up a pin; then he tore 'em.

There was an old lady from Cork
Who tried to teach fishes to walk.
　　When they tumbled down dead
　　She grew weary and said,
"Now I'll try teaching lobsters to talk."

23

A smart little dingo named Rover,
Whilst munching a strawberry pavlova,
  Said, "If this is Down Under,
  Where on earth then I wonder,
Is that marvellous place called Up Over?"

Said an old codger out at Ayers Rock,
Who had swallowed a grandfather clock,
  "The ticking, I find,
  Most people don't mind,
It's the chiming that gives them a shock!"

There was a young girl from Geelong,
Had a penfriend who lived in Hong Kong.
  With every new letter,
  His English got better,
But all of his spelling was wong.

TWO MY VELLY BEST FLEND, HIGH! HOW AH EWE? EYE AM WELL.
          WILLY

There was a strange lady whose spine
Was replaced with a mercury line.
  In wintertime she
  Measured just four foot three,
While in summer she hit six foot nine.

There was a young man from the Bight,
Had a passion for fresh Vegemite.
   He loved it on toast
   But used it the most
For keeping his shoes clean and bright.

26

ANGUS & ROBERTSON PUBLISHERS

Unit 4, Eden Park, 31 Waterloo Road,
North Ryde, NSW, Australia 2113, and
16 Golden Square, London W1R 4BN,
United Kingdom

First published in Australia
by Angus & Robertson Publishers in 1985
First published in the United Kingdom
by Angus & Robertson (UK) in 1985
Reprinted 1988

ISBN 0 207 15019 2

Typeset in 14pt Paladium by Midland Typesetters
Printed in Singapore